The story of Haw
MARDALE
REVISITED

© Geoffrey Berry, 1984
ISBN 0 90 2272 53 5

Printed and Published in England,
by Westmorland Gazette, Kendal.

MARDALE REVISITED
The story of Haweswater

By
GEOFFREY BERRY

With
19 illustrations
and a map.

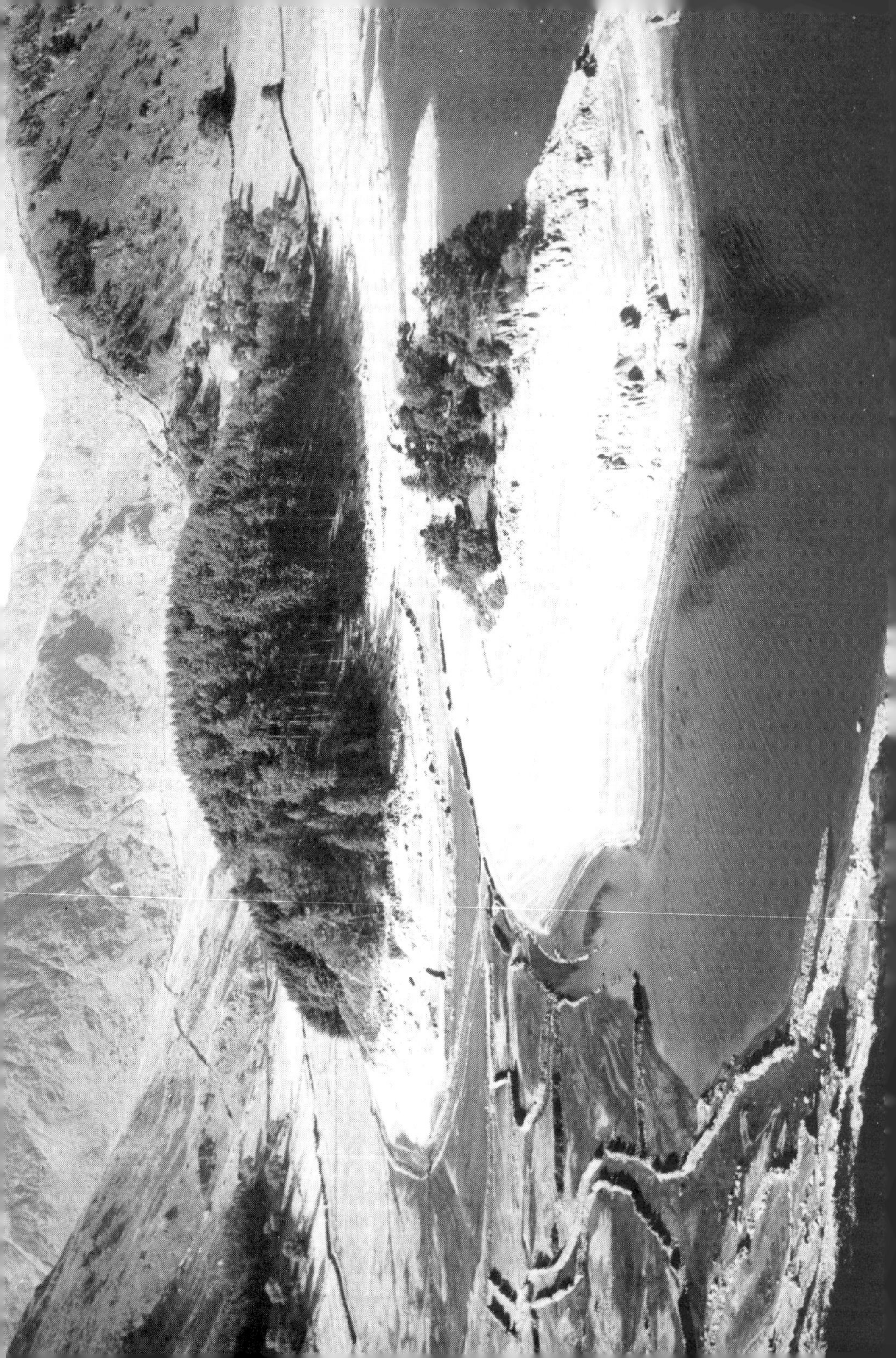

Illustrations

	Page
Haweswater from Whiteacre Crag, 19th July 1984	4
Chapel Bridge revealed	6
Ruins of Chapel Hill and the Church	8
The remains of Goosemire	10
Goosemire before the flooding	12
Mardale in 1934	14
Measand Promontory 1934	16
Measand Promontory 1984	18
Holy Trinity Church, Mardale	22
The last service, 18th August 1935	24
Measand School rebuilt	26
The Dun Bull Hotel	28
Haweswater from Harter Fell	30
The dam, July 1984	32
The draw-off tower	34
Prehistoric standing stones	36
Western shore, Haweswater	37
Blea Water from Harter Fell	38
Castle Crag	39

Old photographs from the files of the Friends of the Lake District. Modern photographs by the author.

Haweswater from Whiteacre Crag on 19th July 1984. Wood Howe island on the right, only its treed crest is normally visible.

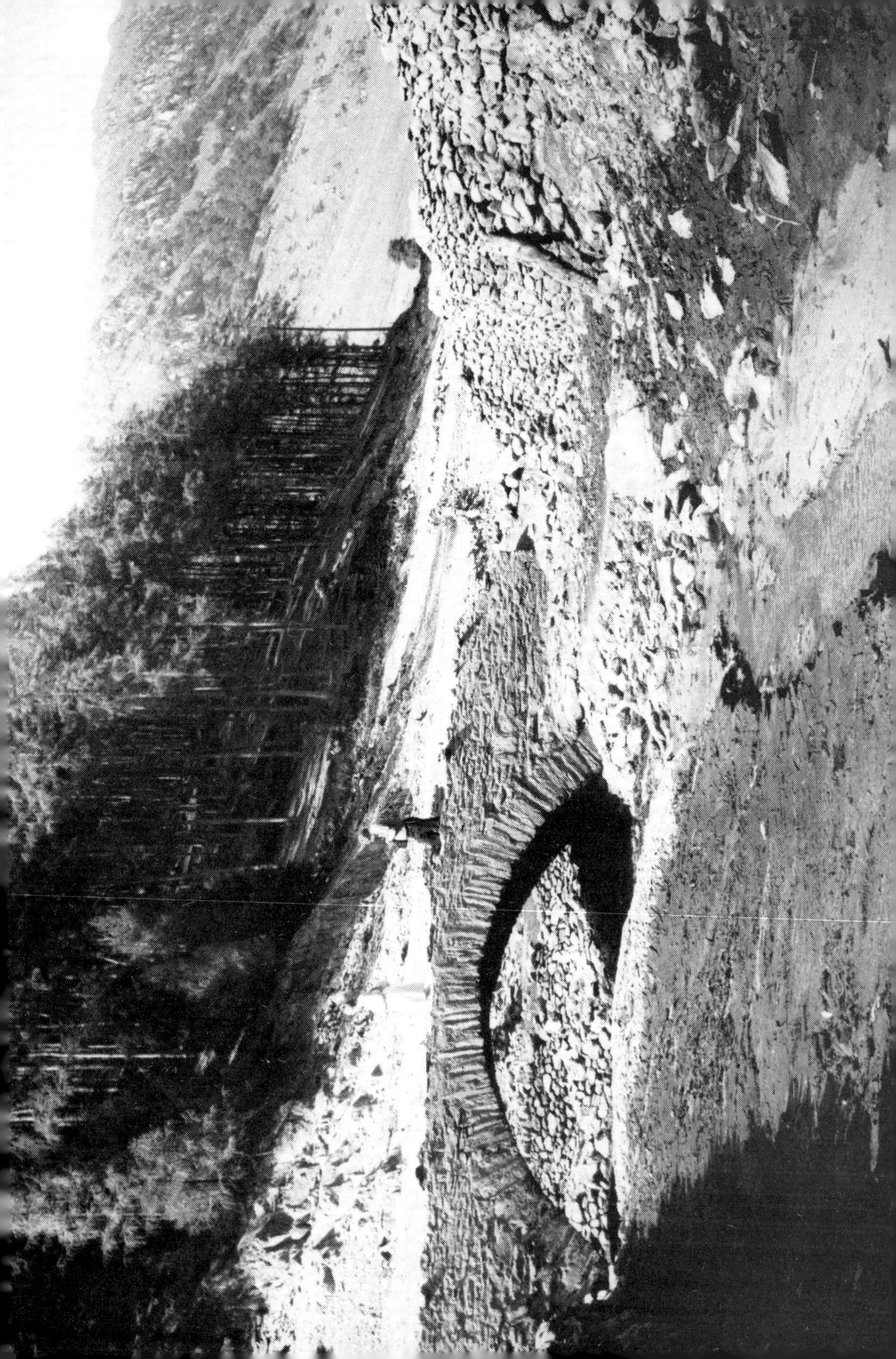

Preface

As I write this little book in the first days of August the sun shines. There has been one day of rain which has made next to no difference to the level of Haweswater. How much longer will the drought last here in the north-west of England? No one knows. There may be heavy or prolonged rain tomorrow or next week. At some time the ruins of Mardale will be covered again, perhaps for many years, perhaps for another fifty years. This book is intended to help all those interested to understand what happened at Mardale, and to ponder a little at what it was like before 1935.

I am grateful for the help I have had from many people. As Consultant Secretary of the Friends of the Lake District I have been fortunate to have access to the Society's records, which have been a rich mine of information in newspaper cuttings, photographs and old maps.

Chapel Bridge over Mardale Beck revealed in the 1984 summer drought.

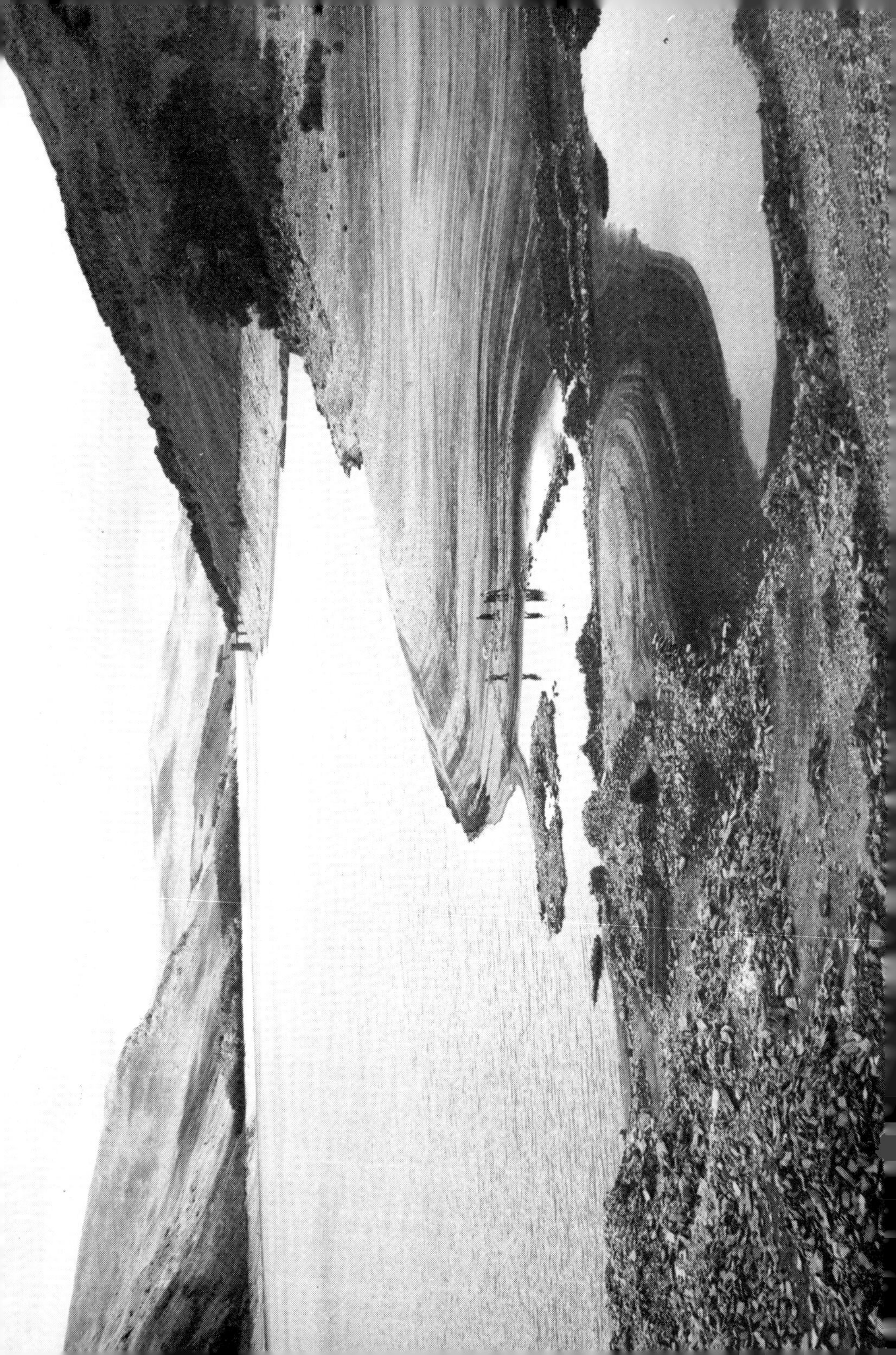

MARDALE REVISITED
July 1984.

In the spring and summer drought of 1984, probably the most severe it was said, for a hundred years, the Haweswater reservoir was drawn down further than it had been since its construction. On the 23rd July the water level was over 37 feet below normal and was falling at the rate of about three feet a week. Less than a million gallons a day was flowing in, as against eighty million going out. A wide white band of bare rock and stones surrounded the whole lake, giving the valley a devastated look. As the waters receded, the remains of the old Mardale were revealed.

All parts of Cumbria showed the effects of the prolonged absence of rain. The fellsides were parched yellow, in the valleys the trees, in dark green leaf, stood out against the pale coloured background. Streams which in living memory had never ceased to flow, dried up, and small tarns in the high hills disappeared. Lake levels fell even where their water was not used for supply purposes and Thirlmere looked half empty and desolate. The Water Authority, perhaps in the belief that rain in the Lake District could not be long delayed, postponed restrictions until the end of June. Then the more extravagent uses were forbidden and every economy urged. By that time Haweswater was well down.

"The most primitive and secluded dale, the most charming and restful to be found in all Lakeland", wrote Councillor Hinchcliffe of Manchester, describing Mardale in 1921, at a time when only the discerning visitor penetrated into the valley. In this summer of 1984 it was all very different. There is a strange fascination in the re-emergence of a drowned village and as soon as this happened in Mardale the valley became a place of pilgrimage. Television crews arrived to film the scene and interview former inhabitants of Mardale now living in the surrounding villages. National newspapers published pictures and carried articles; there were reports and reminiscences on radio. As the water receded even further, there came a different flood — of cars and people, numbering thousands daily. The narrow road to the dale head was jammed with traffic and the limited turning space at the road end became blocked. Ice cream and hot-dog vans added to the chaos. The police were finally obliged to close the road and then to control the numbers allowed in the area. Many people, having had to

In the foreground the ruins of the buildings on Chapel Hill, beyond the remains of the Church are just emerging from the water — 29th June 1984. The bare slope of Wood Howe rises to the right.

9

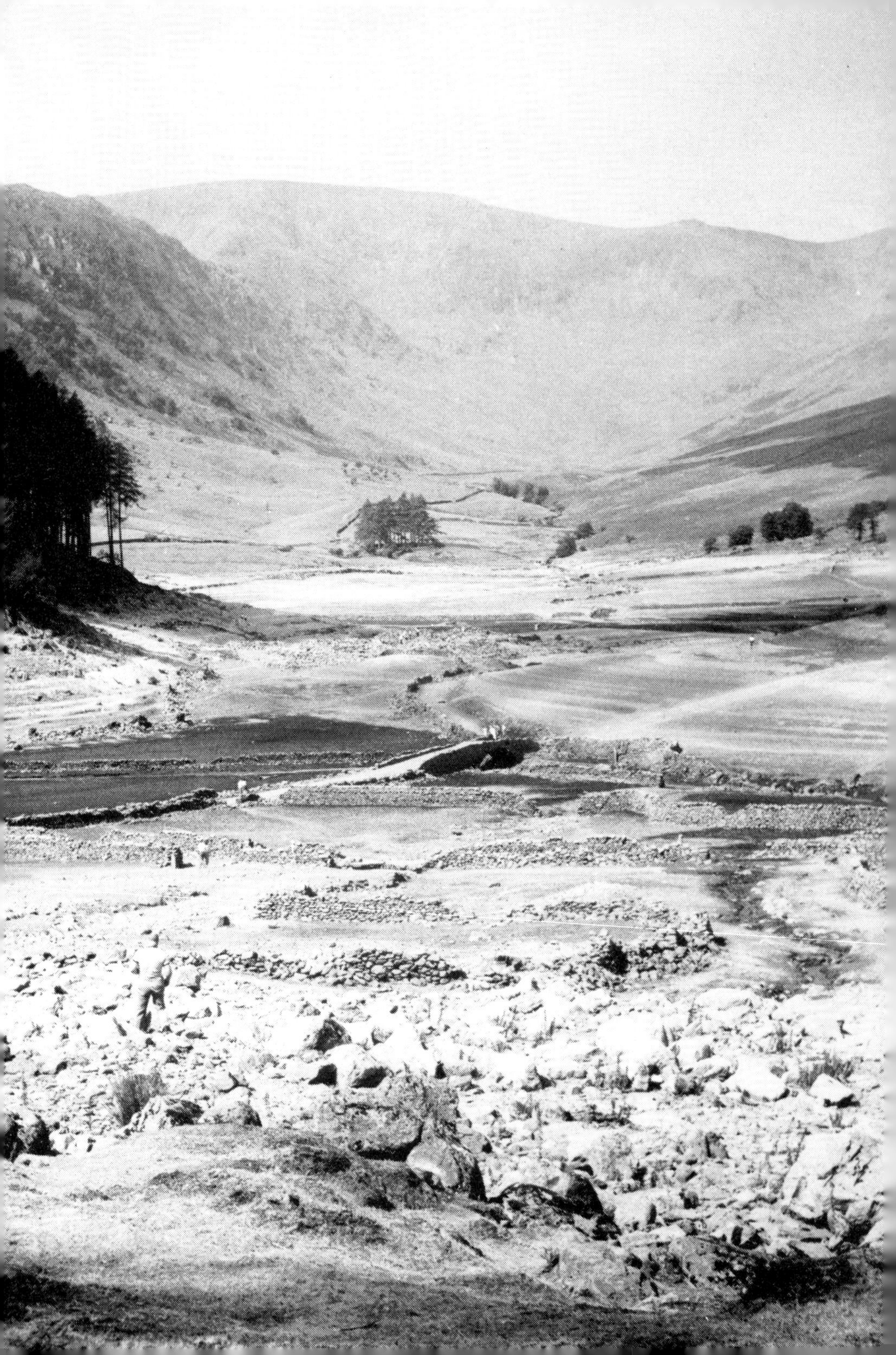

leave their cars far from Mardale Green, walked unaccustomed miles along the road; other more sturdy walkers came over the fells to look down from more peaceful vantage points to the exposed valley floor.

The Drowned Village.

Many who came by the road stopped at its highest point to go through the little gate on to Whiteacre Crag. Here there is a fine viewpoint, but this summer it has looked down on a drained valley floor where the ruins of Mardale have lain like a dismembered skeleton. The boundary walls of the tracks and fields have remained largely intact, but all the former buildings are now heaps of stones. From this viewpoint, Wood Howe, in normal conditions Haweswater's only island showing only a small treed crown, now revealed that it was set upon the broad base of a cone, stark and white. No longer an island, the gulls which had made it their home had flown before the human invasion; they continued to complain loudly at the disturbance. Beyond Wood Howe is the afforested peninsula of the Rigg, and curving round its base the dale road. On the valley floor were the remains, only just distinguishable, of the Dun Bull Inn. Harter Fell stood dramatically at the dale head, with the shoulder of Branstree on the left and Mardale Ill Bell, partially screened by Riggindale's Crags, on the right.

Leaving Whiteacre Crag and going a little further along the road, at another small gate near Hopgill Beck, is the beginning of the footpath to Mardale Head. Many visitors have gone down the steep brackeny hillside here to the bare stoney bed of the reservoir, clambering over the heaps of stones which were once the farms of Goosemire and Grove Brae. Chapel Hill Bridge, built in the seventeenth century, was the only easily recognisable feature. The soft mud and silt which lay, at first, in a deep film over the tracks and bridge, became in the days of hot sunshine and under the tramp of thousands of feet, a surface as hard and smooth as in the days before the flood. Beyond the bridge at the foot of the shingly slope of Wood Howe were the remains of the church, the low piles of stones emphasising how tiny the building was. There were to be seen the stumps of the ancient yews which it is said predated the church and rose higher than its little tower. Across the road from the church was the rubble of the buildings which clustered on Chapel Hill, the little track which wound among them clearly discernable, and here again the sawn butts of the great trees which had sheltered the dwellings.

Looking over the rubble of Goosemire to Chapel Bridge and Chapel Hill into Riggindale — July 1984.

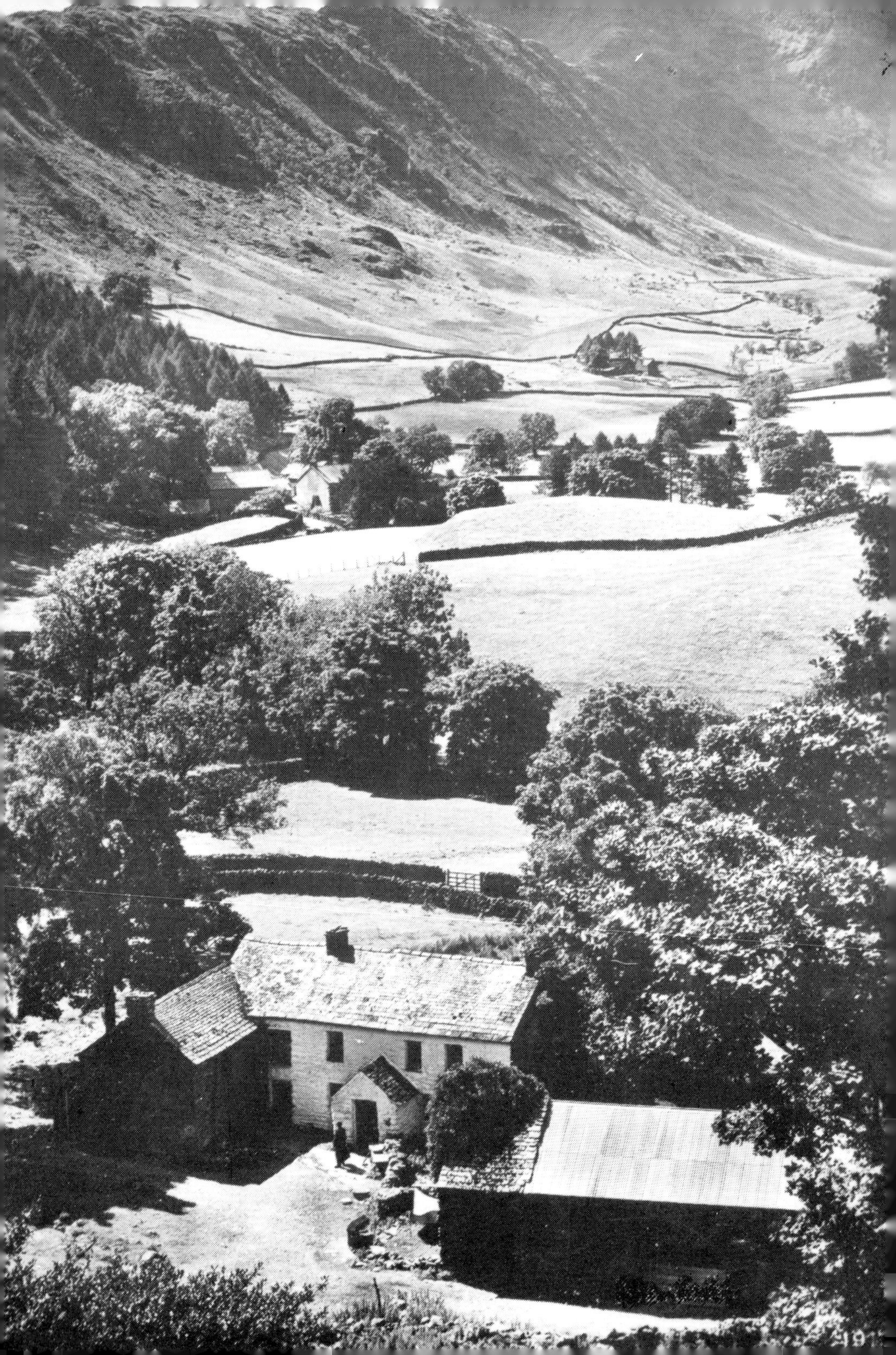
19

Before the Flood

There is no doubt that Mardale was an unspoilt and beautiful valley before the building of the dam. The valley was approached by a narrow twisting road from Bampton, with the slopes of Burnbanks rising gently on the right and the steep craggy mountainside of Naddle Forest across the valley. The pastoral shore of the natural lake, Hawes Water, was just ahead, with stepping stones at the river's outflow. The lake was 2½ miles long, almost divided into two parts by the delta which had been formed over the millenia by the Measand Beck. The smaller and eastern end of the lake was known as Low Water and the western end, beyond Measand, High Water. The narrow connecting isthmus was called The Straights.

The road ran on the west side of the lake following the curving shoreline, providing lovely views across the water to Mardale Common and the dramatic mountains of the dale head. The valley road was bordered with blackthorn, hawthorn, mountain ash, willow, gorse and broom, bramble and wild raspberries. The wayside banks grew primroses and violets, bluebells and meadowsweet; in summer there were foxgloves and wild roses.

Where at Measand the road cut across the peninsula, on the right was Measand Hall standing among great sycamores, near it were the earthworks of a prehistoric fort and, across Measand Bridge, Sandhill and other buildings. Green meadows, stone-walled, sloped down to the lake. All are now gone. The artist Heaton Cooper wrote of a visit to Measand in his book *THE LAKES,* "I don't know whether it was the exceptional beauty of those still autumn days or the knowledge that, in a few years' time, this valley would be under water, that gave our stay at Measand a poignancy that can still affect me over forty years later". He spoke affectionately of Measand Falls "that come down in two tiers with several cascades between steep rocky islands open to the sun and sky". This scene, at least, still remains, as the falls are above the reservoir level; spectacular after heavy rain, they are easily seen from the public road on the other side of the reservoir.

The Old School

A little further up the dale before the head of the lake was reached and where the track went off to Low and High Whelter, stood the school. It was founded in 1713 by Richard Wright, it was a small building with room for not more than a dozen pupils. It too was threatened by the rising water, so the building was carefully

Before the flooding. Goosemire, looking into Riggindale.

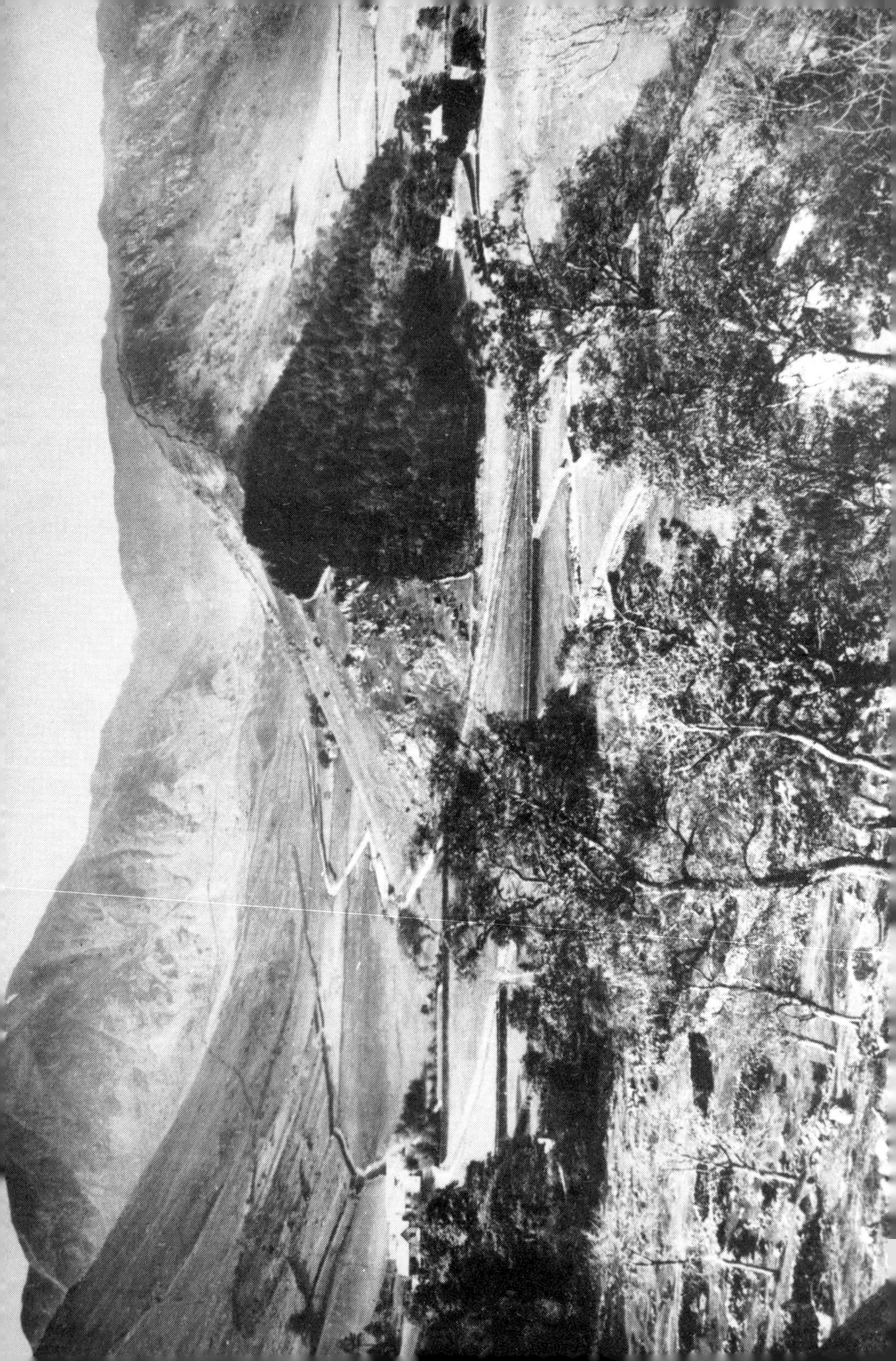

dismantled and rebuilt at Walmgate Head at the expense of a private wellwisher. The reconstructed building, now the private residence of a lady who lived at Measand, is about a mile north of Burnbanks, almost opposite the track to Thornthwaite Hall.

A mile further up the valley, at Mardale Green beyond Riggindale, was the Church. It was to the left of the road and opposite a cluster of buildings on the little eminence known as Chapel Hill lying close under the steep wooded side of the Rigg. The Rigg, now wholly wooded, is the peninsula which stretches into the reservoir waters. Behind the church rose the conical hill, Wood Howe, with its crest of trees; this is now, at normal times, an island.

As the traveller along the dale road continued, the farms of Goosemire and Grove Brae were ahead near the foot of the steep slope down which the Hopgill Beck splashed and tumbled over the rocks. Then the traveller crossed the Mardale Beck by Chapel Bridge and, bearing right, went the few hundred yards to the Dun Bull Inn. Beyond the Inn there was only a walled track, still plainly visible when the lake is low, which led over the Nan Bield Pass into Kentmere, or turning left, over the Gatesgarth Pass into Longsleddale.

Holy Trinity Church, Mardale.

Some six hundred years ago when Shap Abbey was in its prime the monks, it is believed, founded an oratory in Mardale, at Chapel Hill. Towards the end of the 17th century it seemed that the tiny church was built on this same site. The tower was only 29½ feet high. It is said that the six ancient yews which surrounded the church predated it; they grew to be taller than the tower. The sawn stumps of these yews could be plainly seen in this year's drought. At the dissolution of the monasteries, Mardale was included in the parish of Shap.

Until early in the 18th century the dead of Mardale were taken, the coffin strapped to the back of a pack horse, by the Corpse road over Mardale Common and down Swindale for burial at Shap. This entailed a climb to over 1600 feet up a track, still visible and a right of way today, which zig-zags up the steep shoulder of the fell by the spectacular falls of Hopgill Beck. In time the right of burial was granted to Mardale and the first burial there was in 1729.

The last service in the church was held on 18th August 1935 when the congregation far exceeded the capacity of the small church; there

Mardale 1934. The Dun Bull Inn on the left in the middle distance and Chapel Hill and the Church on the right below the afforested Rigg.

15

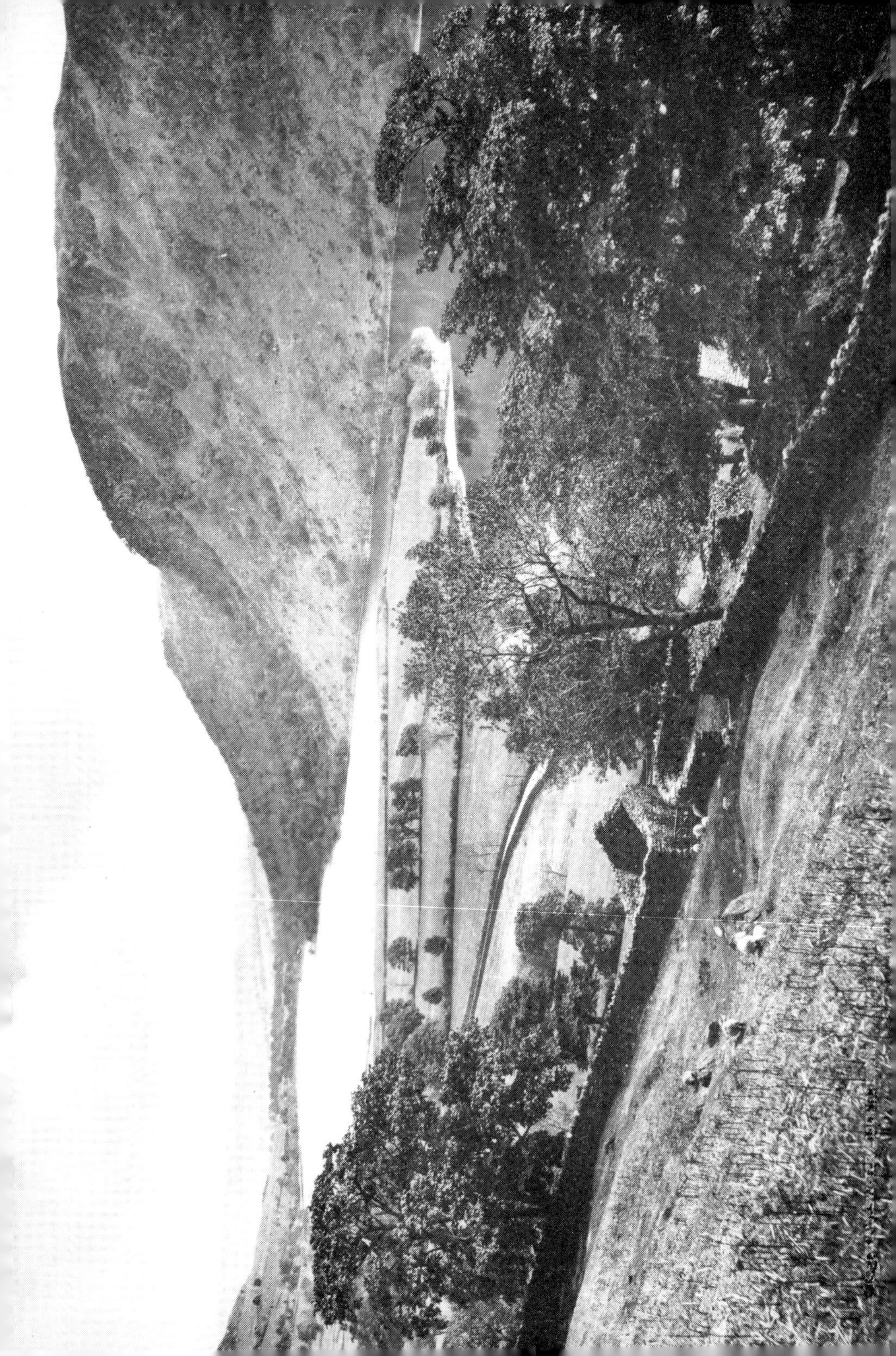

was room for only 75 people and they were admitted by ticket. The Bishop of Carlisle was present. Those outside followed the service, conducted by the Revd. W. H. Cormack, Vicar of the combined parishes of Bampton and Mardale, and the Revd. F. S. Sinker, Vicar of Shap, by loud speakers fixed to the church tower. The psalm sung was "I will lift up mine eyes unto the hills", and the hymns included "O God our Help in Ages Past", "The Church's One Foundation", and "Bright Vision that Delighted", a line which seemed to sum up all the marvellous beauty of the valley.

It is said that the voices of the great congregation rose high into the hills, but that the sheep grazing on the green pastures in the bright sunshine did not for a second cease.

The Bishop, in the sermon, said that they were there that afternoon to perform divine service for what would probably be the last time in that church. They had tried to keep the service as simple as possible and as much like the services which had been performed there for upwards of two hundred years.

The Revd. F. H. J. Barham, then of Newark, was also at this final service. He had been Vicar at Mardale for twenty five years, and that August afternoon he put on his clerical garb but, feeling unable to go into the church for the service, he wandered among the crowd of many thousands, talking to the people who had been his parishioners.

At the close of the service the Bishop offered prayers for all the living descendants of the Holme family, and known as the "Kings of Mardale" who had known and loved this little church. It is said that Hugh Holme, whose ancestors came over with William the Conquerer, was implicated in the Canterbury Conspiracy against King John in 1208. When the plot was discovered he fled to seek safety in Scotland. Avoiding the main routes he came into Mardale and then into Riggindale where he found shelter in a cave on the northern side of Rough Crag; Hugh's Cave is still marked on the large scale maps. Having spent some considerable time in the valley he became so attached to Mardale that he decided to remain there permanently. He became known as the King of Mardale, and the head of the Holme family, down the centuries, succeeded to that title. The last of the male line, Hugh Parker Holme, died in 1885. The family built Bowderthwaite which was at the foot of Riggindale, but other Holmes lived at various times at Chapel Hill and Grove Brae.

The promontory of Measand Beck, 1934, showing the Straits, the narrow strip of water which joined High Water with Low Water. The valley road can be seen in the middle distance and Low Water beyond.

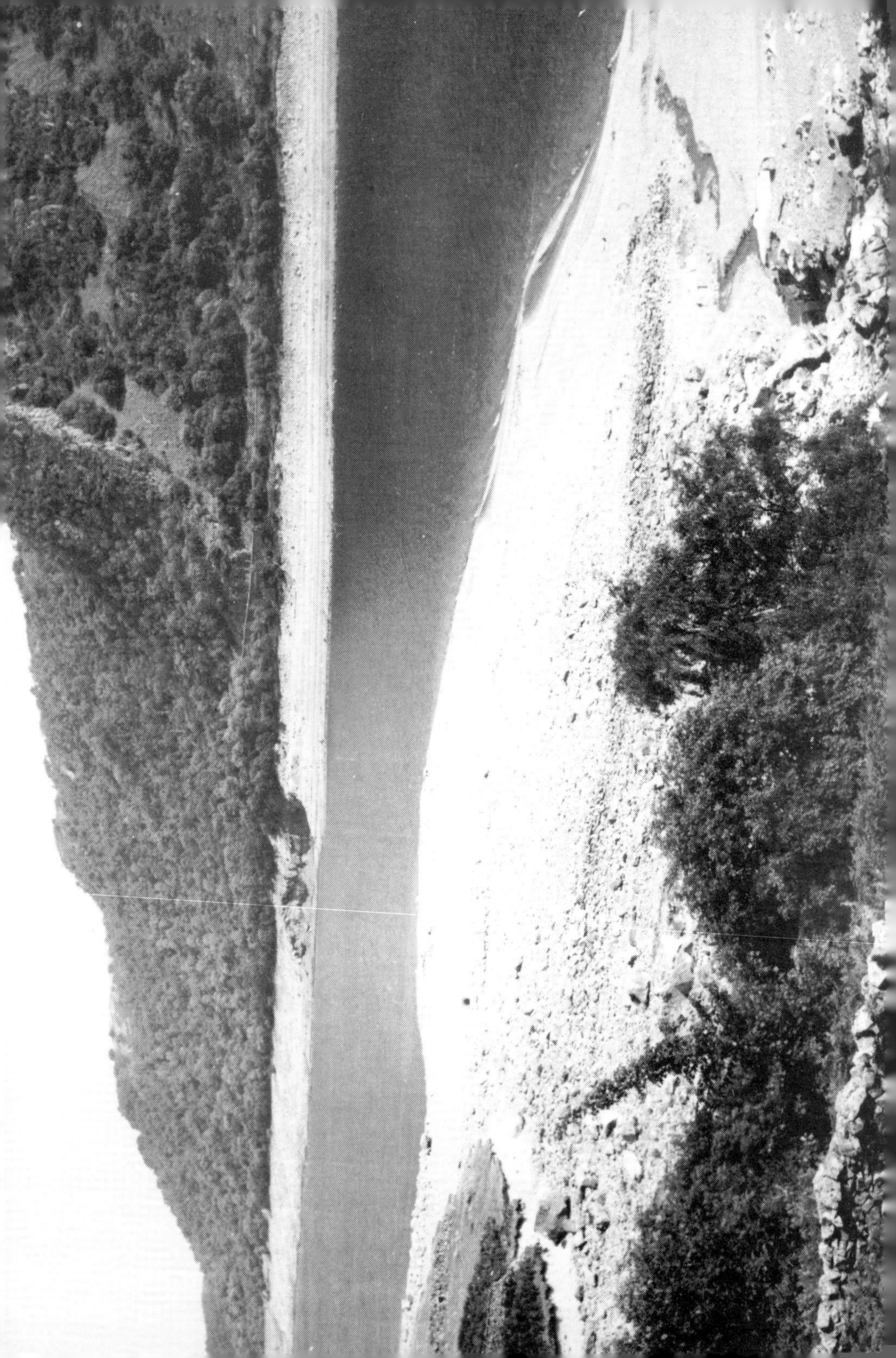

The Church's Contents.

There was strong local feelings about the disposal of Mardale Church furnishings. The churchwardens of Shap, three of whom had been churhwardens for 24 years each, and many of the inhabitants of Mardale and Shap, thought that the contents of the doomed church should go to Shap, which was in any case the mother church. A day-long hearing at a Consistory Court took place also in August 1935, when Chancellor H. B. Vaisey KC heard the application of the Archdeacon of Carlisle that the chief contents of Mardale Church should be removed to the new church of St, Barnabas at Carlisle, then in course of erection. Mr. Q. L. W. Little, solicitor of Penrith, objected to the proposal as the lineal descendent of the Holmes of Mardale; he also represented the Shap churchwardens in their objection. In the day-long proceedings many interested matters where raised. The Chancellor asked Mr. Little whether Shap would want the weather vane and the Mardale bell; the weather vane was said to be one of the most valued relics. Mr. Hindon, one of the wardens, was asked whether they really wanted two pulpits at Shap; he replied that the new church was to have two pulpits, so why not Shap? When the fate of the Mardale font was under discussion the then Vicar of Shap, the Rev. F. S. Sinker, was asked whether Shap wanted it; he replied, "We have three already". The decision of the Court was that the main contents of the Mardale Church should go to the new Carlisle Church. However, not all of it did so, the Jacobean oak pulpit is in use today in Borrowdale Church at Rosthwaite.

Mardale Church was demolished in 1936. About one hundred coffins from the churchyard were exhumed and taken to a cemetery at Shap which is separate from the churchyard, lying just east of Shap Church beyond the railway line. A walled section of the cemetery is reserved for the tombstones and other plaques from Mardale.

Although the Church Authorities were paid compensation by Manchester Corporation of £2405 for the church, parsonage and a small glebe, it was believed on the understanding that a new church would be built, this did not happen. Emotional letters were written to the newspapers complaining that, while nothing was being done about a new church, steps were being taken to replace the Dun Bull Inn and to rebuild the school.

The Measand Promontory, July 1984. The beck can be seen running out on the right. Across the water, normally below water level, are quarries from which material was obtained for the dam and new road. Above, Naddle Forest and to the right Wallow Crag.

MARDALE
Hawes Water – then and now

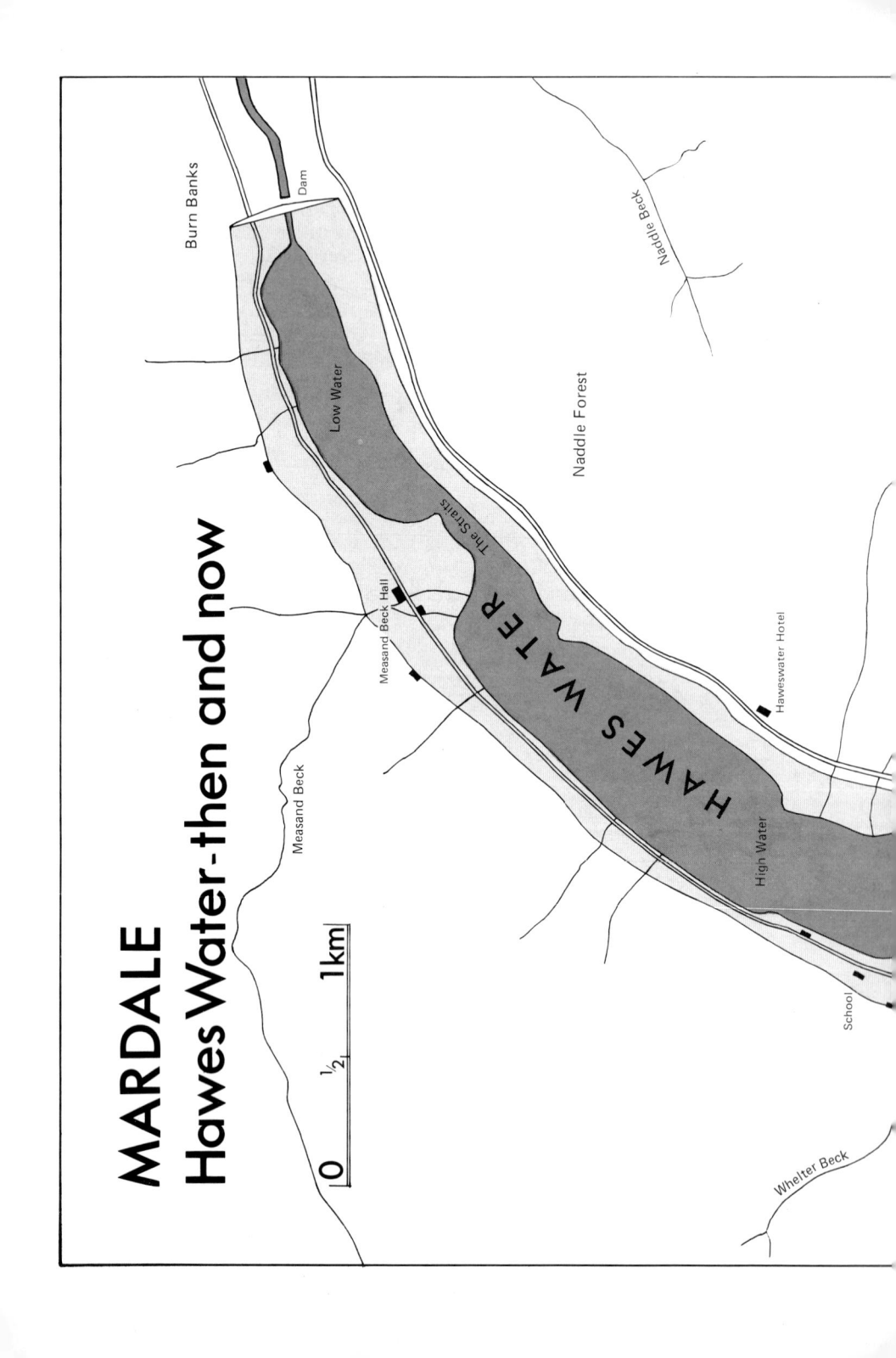

MARDALE

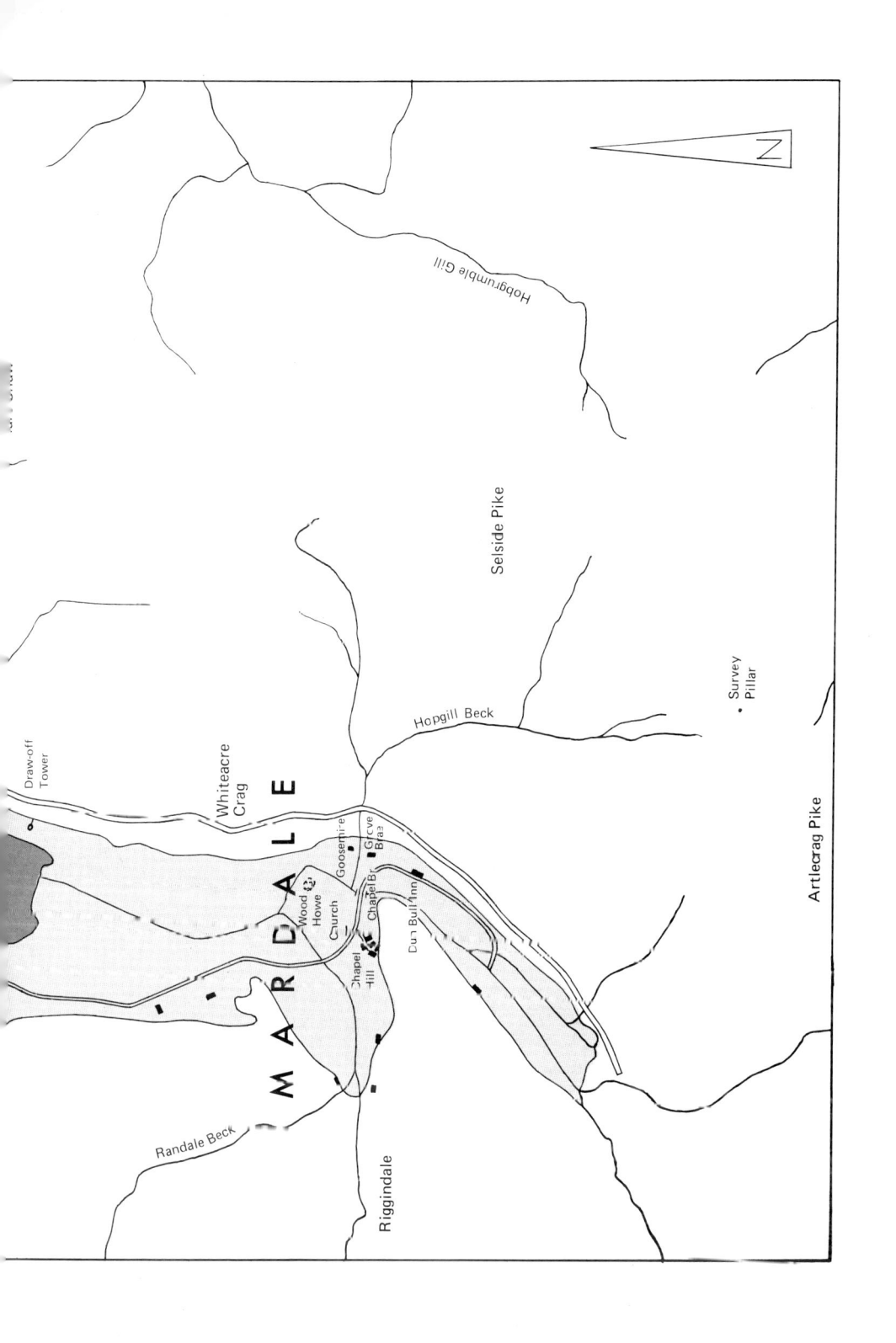

Draw-off Tower
Whiteacre Crag
Wood Howe
Church
Chapel Hill
Chapel Br
Goosemire
Grove Brae
Dun Bull Inn
Randale Beck
Riggindale
Hopgill Beck
Hopgrumble Gill
Selside Pike
Survey Pillar
Artlecrag Pike

N

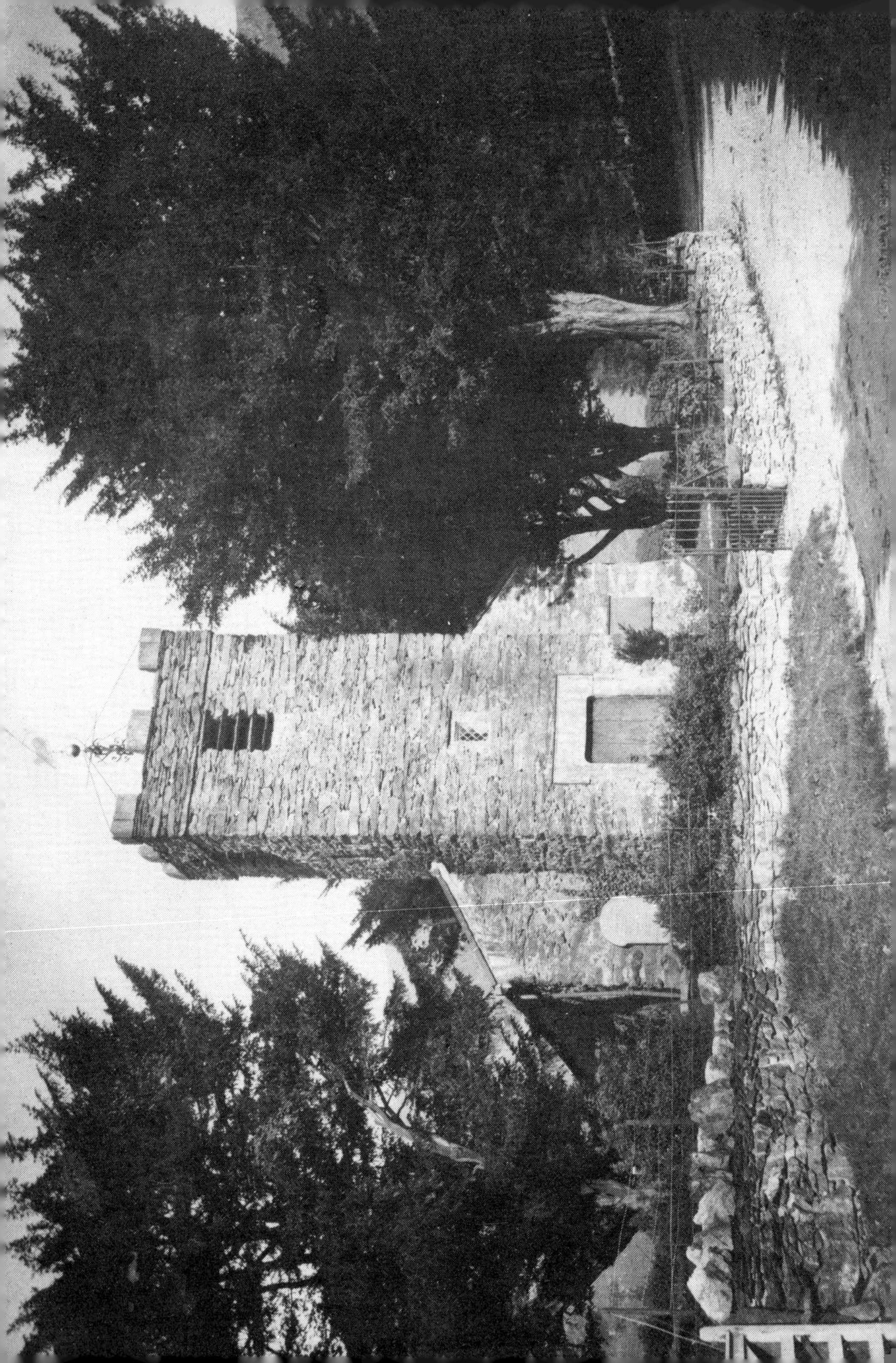

The Dun Bull Inn and the Haweswater Hotel

The Dun Bull stood at the meeting place of the hill tracks. There appears to have been a hostelry hereabouts for four or five hundred years. Like many old Lakeland inns it combined farming with its functions as an inn. It had a few rooms for summer visitors and those who came to fish and climb throughout the year. Its fame as the centre for the Mardale Shepherd's Meets was widespread.

Manchester Corporation undertook to provide an hotel in its place when the valley was flooded, though many of the reports at the time refer to the new building being a 'rest house', which seems a strange term to use. The siting and design of the new hotel was a source of prolonged controversy. At first it was suggested that it should be near the summit of the Rigg, as it was argued that it would then meet the needs of travellers crossing the fells on the various tracks. It is hard to see now how the Rigg site would have been convenient unless the dale road on the western side of the lake, due to be flooded, was realigned at a higher level; this indeed was a possibility at one time. Councillor Hinchliffe thought the Rigg site ideal, contending that it would have enabled expeditions, between breakfast and lunch, to Blea Tarn and Small Water and any one of the dale head's major peaks. The site later chosen for the new hotel was on the east side of the lake, about a mile and a half beyond the dam along the new road. The building was to be set on an elevated shelf below Guerness Woods with extensive views across the lake to the sweeping hillsides rising to the High Street ridge. One problem was the disposal of sewage from so remote a site; now a pipeline carries the hotel's drainage for treatment to a point below the dam.

Even when the new site had been agreed the design of and the materials for the new hotel gave rise to even more dissension. The Council for the Preservation of Rural England thought that the design was totally unsuitable to the traditions of the Lake District and would create an eyesore in Mardale. The Council said that in its view "Instead of a long, low, two-storeyed building in local white wash (the Swan Inn at Grasmere is an excellent example) this casino-like structure will dominate the landscape, a lasting disgrace to its perpetrators". There were consultations with the leading architects who were members of Manchester's Civic Advisory Committee. The Haweswater Hotel we see today, set high above the road, with walled and terraced gardens, was the final result of the years of argument and dozens of letters to the press. Of course, it still did not please everyone.

Holy Trinity Church, Mardale. Its tower was only 29½ feet high.

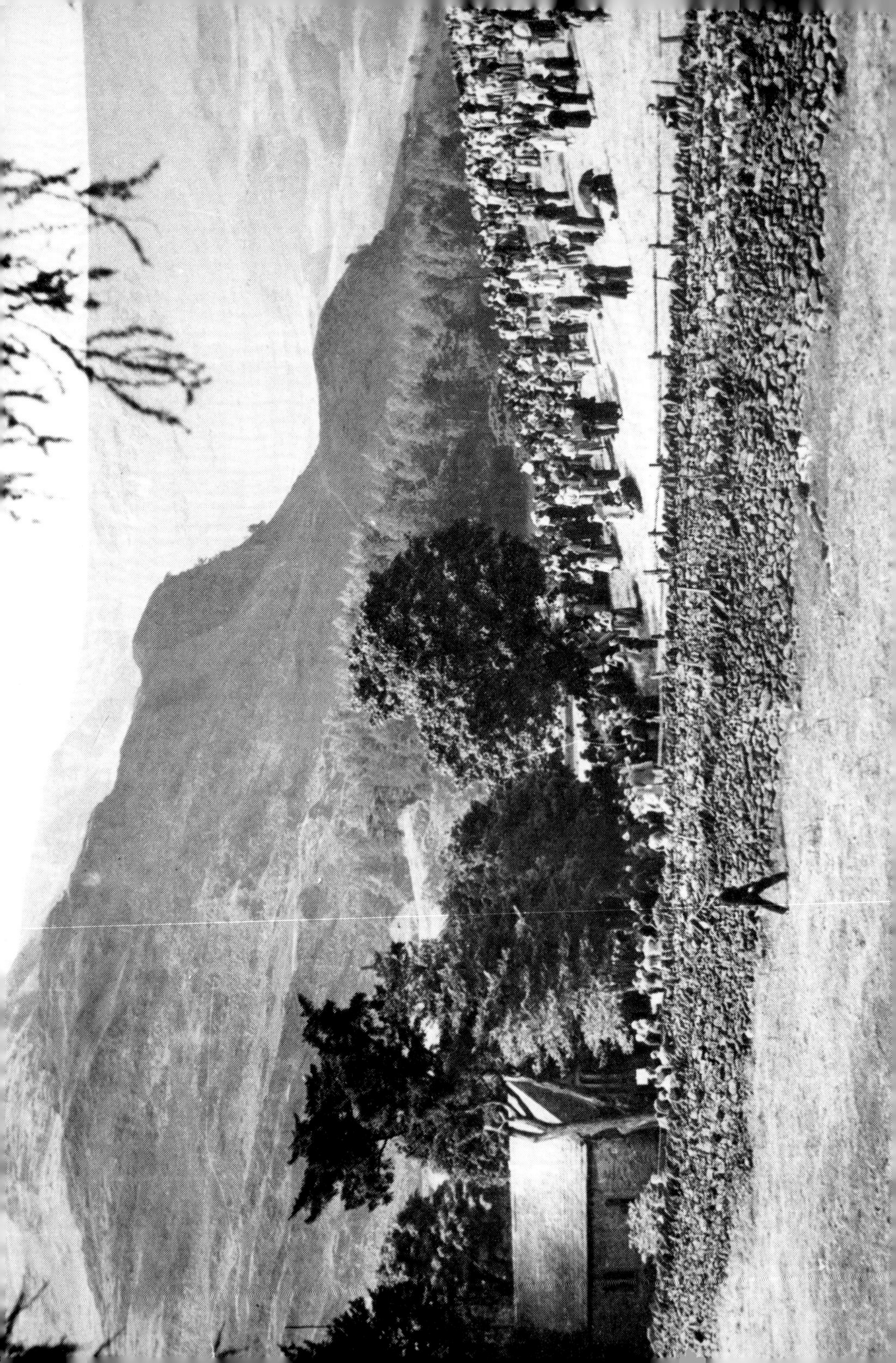

Farming in Mardale.

Sheep had been the mainstay of Mardale farmers for centuries and farming had gone on largely unchanged. A description of life in the dale one hundred and fifty years ago tells of the huge chimneys and fireplaces inside the houses, where meat was suspended to dry for winter consumption and the family gathered for warmth and comfort. The women would sit in this smoky enclave knitting or spinning wool or flax, the men carding the wool, the schoolboy studying his Latin and the old men telling tales of Border strife or ancient legends of the dale. The men wore clothes of native fleece, homespun and woven by the village weaver, the womens were made from finer wool. The salvation of the small farms was the extensive fell pasturage for the sheep and fell ponies. When it was a bad year for sheep there were hard times, in those days there were no EEC subsidies or Ministry of Agriculture grants. There were complaints that the deer from Martindale and Forests in severe weather made predatory excursions on the pastures and crops, but as one old farmer said, "A lot more comes over nor goes back".

Mardale Shepherds' Meet.

Mardale was certainly famous for its autumnal shepherd's meet. Stray sheep were brought from the surrounding fells to be restored to their rightful owners. They were, and still are, identified by their ear and wool markings, each farm having a distinct code. If sheep were not claimed at the local meet it was usual to send them on to other meets in the area, and if they were still not identified, tradition had it that they were to be kept for a year before they could be sold to defray the expenses of their keep. The ear markings and the wool markings, which had to be renewed every year after clipping, were generally strokes of red, blue or black. The various markings were, and are, complicated enough for a farmer to say, "T'combinations are like t'perms in t'footba' pools".

The original Mardale meets are said to have been held on High Street where in addition to the first purpose of identifying and claiming stray sheep, there was horse racing along the route of the Roman road, wrestling, and other sports. At some time long ago the meets were transferred to the Dun Bull Inn. For example in November 1927 over seven hundred people attended the meet, participating in the hunt with the Ullswater Foxhounds, watching the

The last service at the tiny Mardale Church on 18th August 1935. Only 75 people were able to be inside.

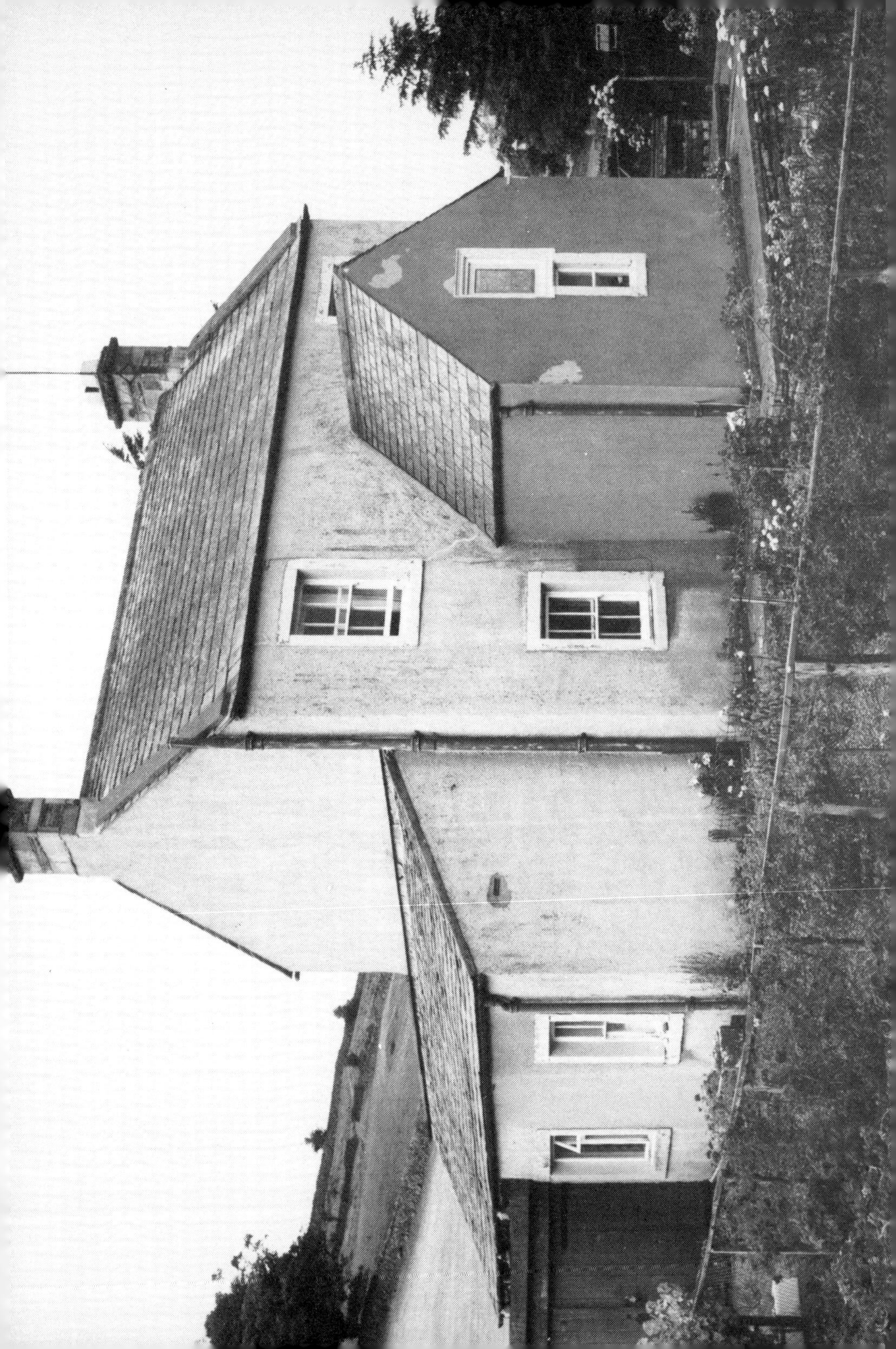

stray sheep being brought down from the fells, taking part in clay pigeon shooting and joining in the festivities of the evening.

The last meet was held in 1935. On that occasion there were many nostalgic tales of earlier meets, recalling times at the Dun Bull when the festivities continued from Friday evening until Tuesday.

The meet is now held in Bampton every November and is attended by farmers from the Mardale Fells, Martindale, Patterdale, Troutbeck, Kentmere, Longsleddale, Shap, Helton and Bampton.

The Reservoir Scheme

Manchester Corporation, the Waterworks Authority at the time, obtained the Haweswater Act in 1919, this gave it powers to acquire the lake in Mardale and the large surrounding catchment area for a major reservoir. The scheme was to be developed in stages, and included works to divert water from neighbouring catchment areas. It also empowered the construction of subsidiary reservoirs in Swindale and Wet Sleddale, the water from these to be taken into the main Haweswater reservoir. The Wet Sleddale reservoir was completed in 1966 but the Swindale reservoir has not been built.

Hawes Water the natural lake of Mardale, was the highest of the English Lakes, being 694 feet above sea level, and this was an important consideration when the water had to be taken to consumers eighty or ninety miles away. Work on the building of the dam started in 1930 but was suspended about a year later because of the national financial crisis. Consideration was given to going ahead with a much smaller scheme involving a dam only 15 feet high, but that proposal was finally rejected. In 1934 work on the original scheme was restarted; it was estimated to cost £12 million.

The dam is 96 feet high and 1550 feet long. It is of the hollow massive-buttress type and embodied features which were unique in Britain at the time of its construction. The reservoir has a capacity of about 18,600 million gallons and a top water level of 790 feet above sea level. The surface area of the full reservoir is three times as great as the size of the natural lake it replaced. The average rainfall over the catchment area is about 75 inches, and the safe reliable yield from the

Measand School, Mardale, dismantled before the flood and rebuilt at Walmgate Head, just north of Burnbanks. The plaque over the porch window reads

"Richard Wright :
Richard Law 1713 :
Founder : Benefactor".

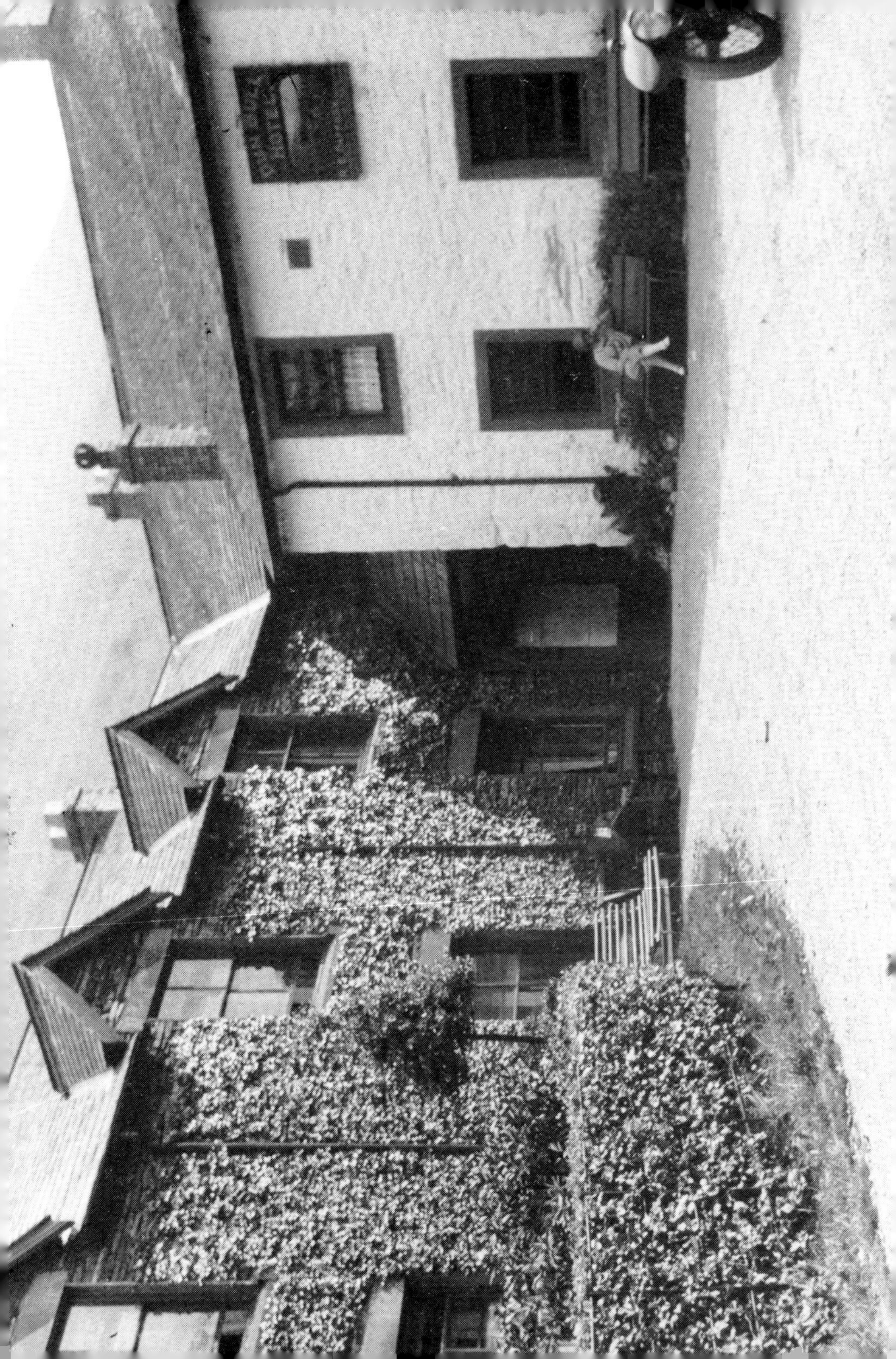

Haweswater scheme is 66 million gallons a day after allowing for the provision of compensation water into the River Lowther.

Some of the stone for the dam and for the new road was quarried in the valley, but so that the workings would not scar the valley, below what was to be the new high water level. Two of these quarries were revealed in July 1984 just below the road near Wallow Crag; anyone paddling into the lake at this point would have had quite a shock, as there is a cliff-like drop.

Tower and Tunnel

The reservoir's water is drawn off through the tower which stands on the shore about half a mile beyond the hotel. Its windows, and most of its stone, came from the demolished Church. There was much concern on the part of the amenity bodies that this building would be inappropriate in its isolated and exposed position, and the trees which are now between the lake and the road were planted as a screen. It is a thrilling experience to go inside the draw-off tower where the water roars far below into the pipeline, filling the confined space with clouds of spray and deafening noise.

From the tower an aquaduct goes first by the Mardale tunnel 1660 feet under Branstree to Longsleddale. At the time it was built this was the longest water tunnel in Britain, requiring 250 tons of gelignite for the blasting work. At Stockdale in Longsleddale there are still spoil heaps of extracted material at the tunnel's emergence. The aquaduct goes on by pipeline underground along the eastern slopes of Longsleddale, though now there is little sign of it.

Near the summit of Artlecrag Pike there is a tall, pillar-like, stone construction which was used in the survey for the pipeline. There is another of these strange constructions on Great Howe north of Stockdale.

In 1934 the pipeline was connected at Garnett Bridge, at the lower end of Longsleddale, to the Thirlmere Aquaduct. This was to enable the Haweswater supply to be used before the rest of the pipeline to Manchester was built. Further progress southwards from Garnett Bridge of the Haweswater pipeline was delayed by the Second World War, and was not resumed until 1948. Now the water from the Haweswater system passes through the Watchgate Treatment Plant, near Kendal, on its way south.

The Dun Bull Inn.

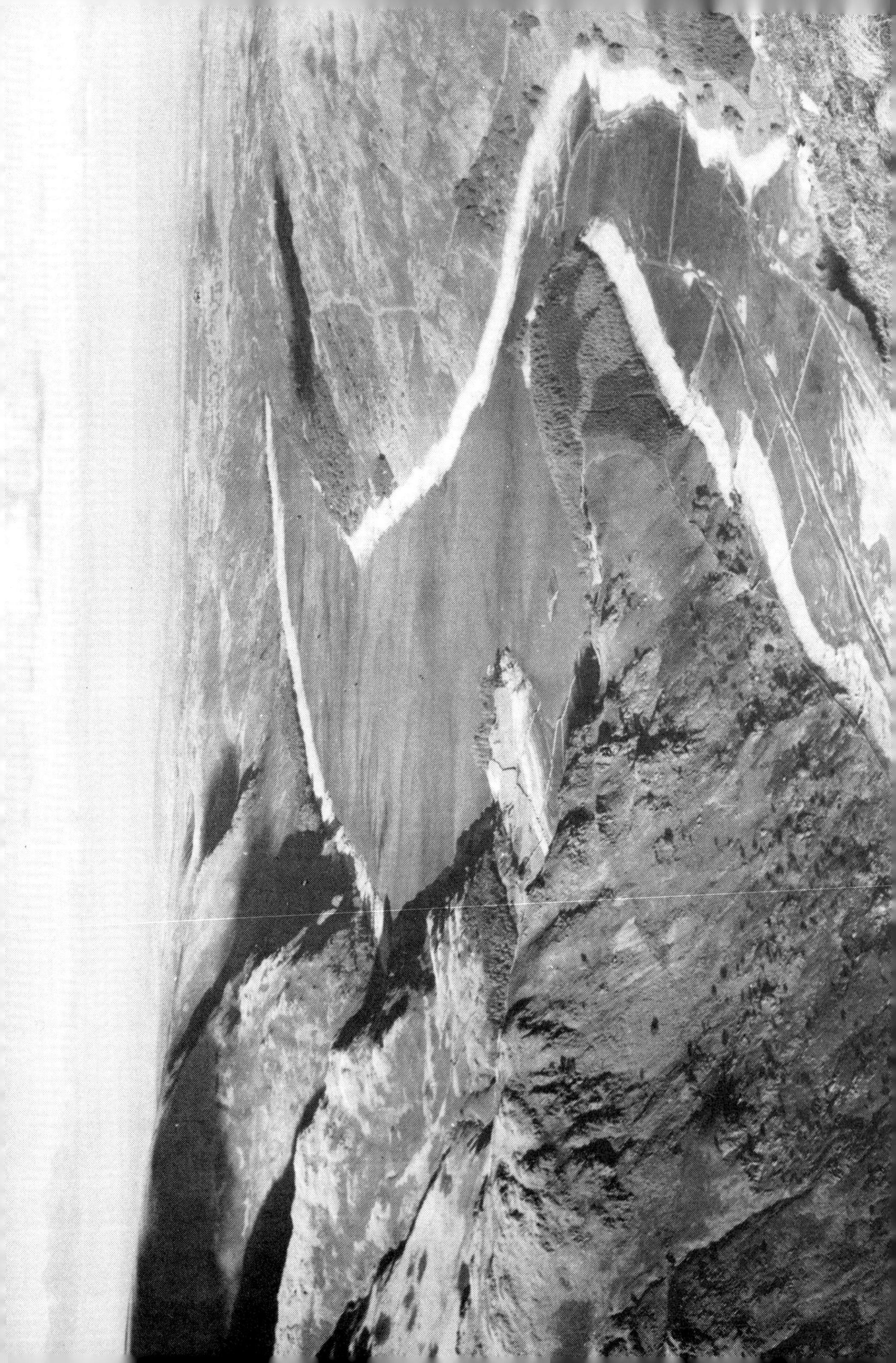

Burnbanks

At the very beginning of the Haweswater construction a number of small bungalows were built at Burnbanks, until then an almost bare fellside, to house two hundred men working on the tunnel and the dam. Many of these houses are still occupied, now cloaked in leafy surroundings.

The Haweswater scheme required the building of a new road to replace the old narrow curving road which ran along the west shore of the lake and which would be flooded by the rising water. Eventually it was decided that the new access road would be on the other, east, side of the valley, cutting along the steep slope through Naddle Forest. There was considerable criticism of this route, as it was contended that its straight line, embanked in places and its boundary walls would create an unnatural scar visible even from High Street. Its width of 24 feet was held to be quite unnecessary for a road, it was said, which would never have to carry much traffic. On the west side of the reservoir a footpath was provided, today an attractive route to the valley head and beyond, as well as being a link in Wainwright's popular 'Coast to Coast' route. Manchester also built a private concrete road across the open moorland to connect with Shap Granite works to bring materials to the dam site. This is still in use today, but is not a right of way.

In the earliest days of the Haweswater project extensive afforestation of the catchment area was contemplated, presumably in pursuance of a policy similar to that which had been carried out at Thirlmere. Undertakings were given that there would not be planting around Blea Tarn and Small Water; fortunately nothing came of the afforestation scheme.

In 1973 when the new water authorities were set up, Manchester Corporation Water Undertaking was transferred to the North West Water Authority. Manchester retained only the Haweswater Hotel which is still managed by the Corporation. It is the only habitation in Mardale beyond the dam.

Haweswater from Harter Fell — May 1984.

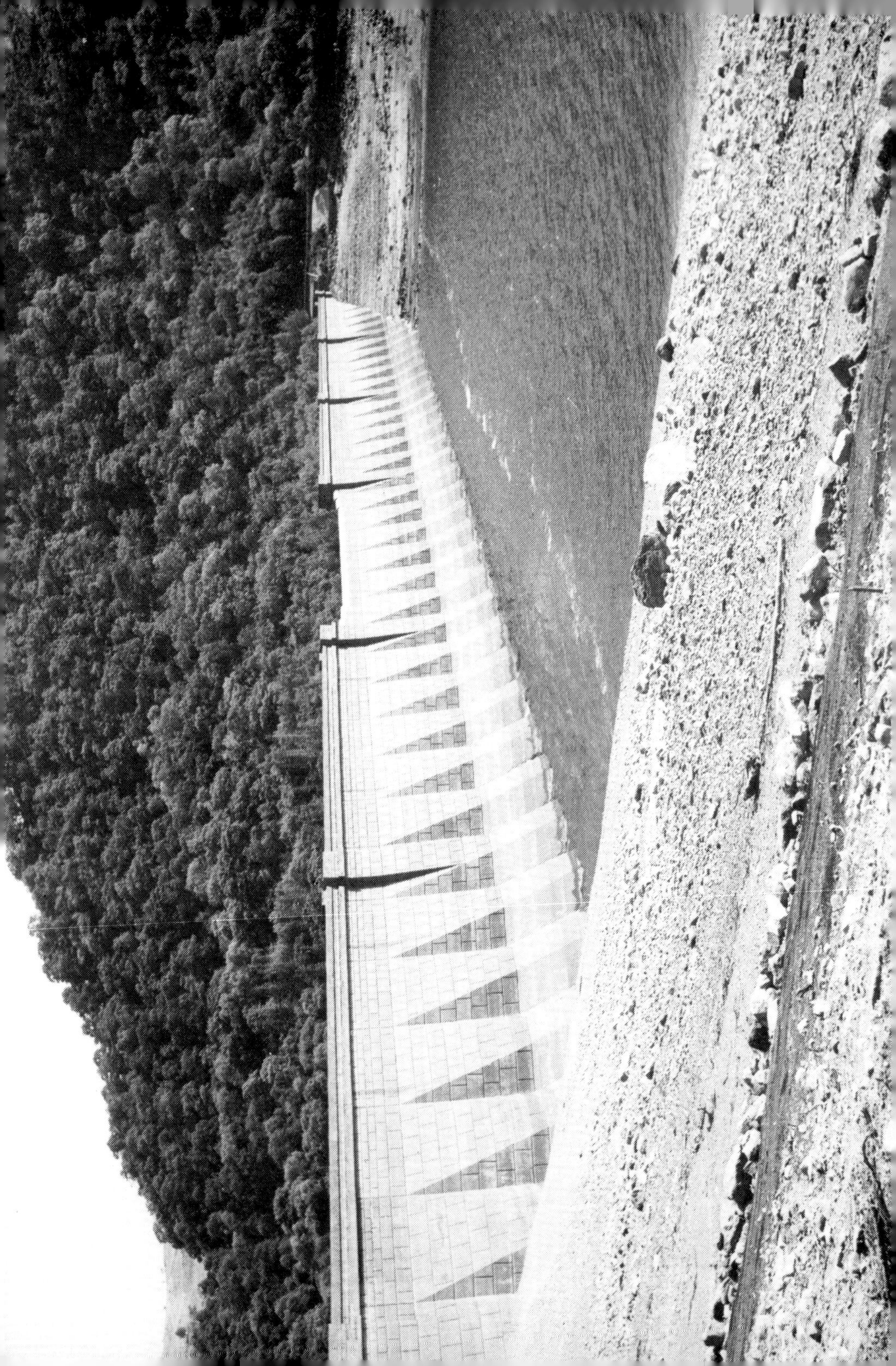

The Valley Now

Above Haweswater there remains a wild, interesting and dramatic countryside. On the western side of the lake there are ancient burial cairns on the rocky bracken-covered slopes, and here also are two prehistoric standing stones from which there is a fine view of the lake and the valley head. There are unfrequented routes on to the High Street ridge by, for instance, the Measand Beck and the upper waterfalls of Fordingdale Force. Randale Beck, running into Haweswater near Riggindale Foot, also has its lovely waterfalls. There is a good walk by Measand End and Long Grain, around the steep head of Whelter Bottom, to the early British Fort on Castle Crag, a lovely place to idle in the warm sunshine of a spring or summer day. Many people traverse the rounded shoulder of Kidsty Pike, and many the rocky narrow ridge of Rough Crag; they are both good routes to and from High Street.

Blea Water in its craggy bowl is the deepest tarn in the Lake District, 207 feet, a mysterious place, its geological origins uncertain. It has been graded a Site of Special Scientific Interest. Small Water, a lovely mountain tarn, lies beside the bridleway from Haweswater over the Nan Bield Pass to Kentmere; close to its shore are small stone shelters, it is not known when or by whom they were built. Harter Fell stands a great sentinel overlooking the flooded valley, its dark rocky northern face streaked with snow-filled gullies for long winter months. There are splendid mountain scenes from the summit, with Blea Water in its deep hollow close under the precipitous eastern face of High Street's long ridge. Below, to the east of Harter Fell, the Gatesgarth Pass carries the bridleway which has for centuries linked Mardale with Longsleddale. The fells beyond, Branstree and Selside Pike, are less contoured sweeping masses of lonely moorland. There is good walking north of the Mardale-Swindale Corpse road, crags and little rocky tops tempt the explorer onwards. Gills with waterfalls tumble down the steep side into the reservoir; foaming torrents after heavy rain, in July 1984 mere trickles linking still dark pools.

The Future

The extent to which recreation should be encouraged and catered for at Haweswater has been much discussed by the Water Authority, the National Park Authority and the statutory and voluntary bodies concerned with conservation. In the mid-seventies there were proposals for boating on the lake from a centre near Measand.

The dam, July 1984, looking towards Naddle Wood.

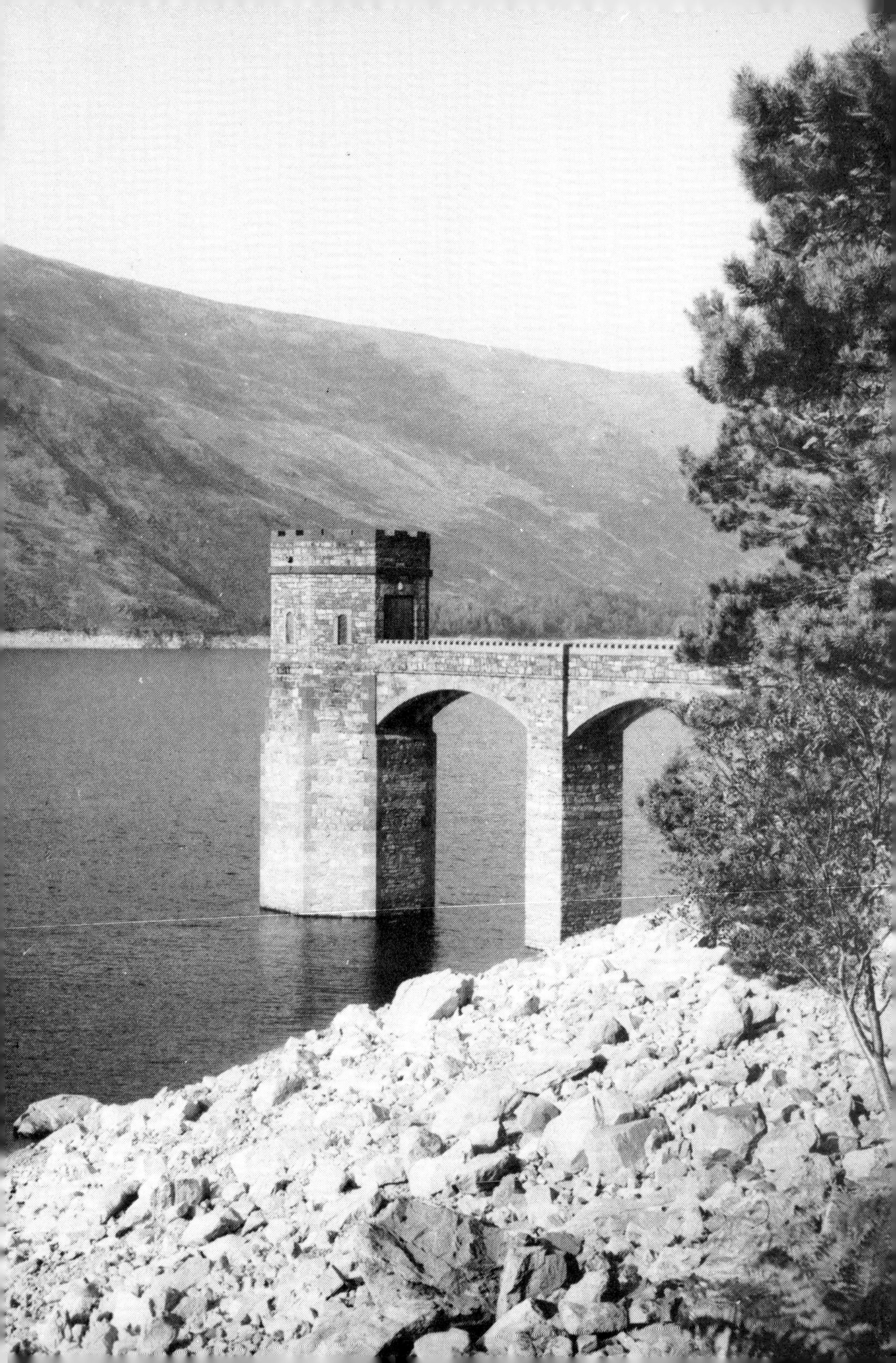

entailing a new road for some distance along the shore, some buildings and slipways. This scheme was fortunately abandoned as being inconsistent with the quiet and underdeveloped nature of the western shore. In any case the great variation in water levels to which Haweswater is subject make it unsuitable and unattractive for boating. This was the experience at Thirlmere when the lake was opened in the summer of 1984 to sailing dinghies for trial periods. The drawn down lake had little recreational use.

Haweswater has still an abundance of wild life; there are forty breeding species of woodland birds at Naddle, including pied flycatcher, wood warbler and redstart. In the mountainous head of the valley there are large birds of prey. Red deer and fell ponies roam the fells, particularly to the west of the lake. There is a rich flora, stretches of juniper scrub, and heather moorland. The pastures and meadows, the oaks and elms, yews and sycamores of the valley floor have gone, but there still remains a wild and beautiful countryside around and above the reservoir to be cared for and enjoyed.

The draw-off tower; its windows and much of the stone came from the demolished church.

The prehistoric standing stones on Bampton Common; looking over a brimming Haweswater to the mountainous head of Mardale.

The footpath on the western shore of Haweswater in winter.

Blea Water from Harter Fell, with High Street in the background and the Riggindale ridge on the right.

Castle Crag in the centre of the picture; on its summit against the sky the remains of an early British Fort.

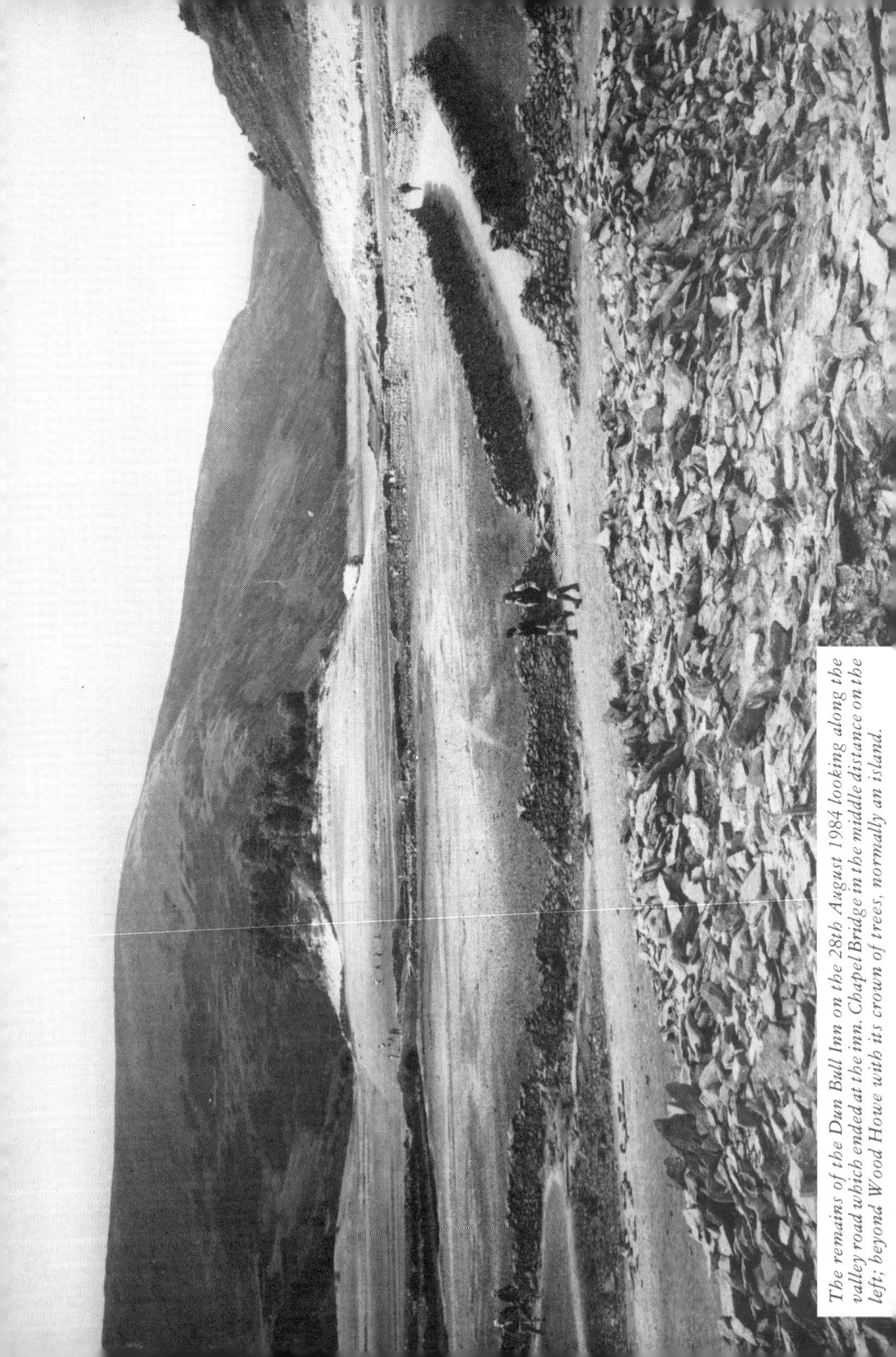

The remains of the Dunn Bull Inn on the 28th August 1984 looking along the valley road which ended at the inn. Chapel Bridge in the middle distance on the left; beyond Wood Howe with its crown of trees, normally an island.